THE EASTERN FRONT

The Germans and Soviets at
War in World War II

BATTLE BRIEFINGS

THE EASTERN FRONT

The Germans and Soviets at War in World War II

Edited by Robert J. Edwards
with contributions by Michael Olive

STACKPOLE
BOOKS
celebrating **90** *years*
Guilford, Connecticut

STACKPOLE
BOOKS

Published by Stackpole Books
An imprint of The Rowman & Littlefield Publishing Group, Inc.
4501 Forbes Blvd., Ste. 200
Lanham, MD 20706
www.rowman.com

Distributed by NATIONAL BOOK NETWORK
800-462-6420

British Library Cataloguing in Publication Information available

Library of Congress Cataloging-in-Publication Data available

ISBN 978-0-8117-1994-0 (paperback)
ISBN 978-0-8117-6784-2 (e-book)

♾™ The paper used in this publication meets the minimum requirements of
American National Standard for Information Sciences—Permanence of Paper for
Printed Library Materials, ANSI/NISO Z39.48-1992.

Printed in the United States of America

Contents

Phase 1:
German Dominance
1

Phase 2:
Strategic Dominance in the Balance
35

Phase 3:
Soviet Dominance
65

Series Introduction

FOR MORE THAN NINETY YEARS, STACKPOLE BOOKS has been publishing the very best in military history, from ancient Rome to the modern Middle East, from foxhole to headquarters. We are proud to draw on that rich heritage—our decades of experience and expertise— in publishing this brand-new series, Battle Briefings. Intended as short overviews, these books aim to introduce readers to history's most important battles and campaigns— and, we hope, to provide a launching pad for further exploration of the endlessly fascinating nooks and crannies of military history.

Introduction

TODAY, ALMOST THREE-QUARTERS of a century after the guns fell silent in May 1945, the term "Eastern Front" still invokes a certain fascination among both the general public and those interested in military history. For sheer size, scope, and complexity, the Russo-German war from 22 June 1941 until 9 May 1945 has never had an equal. It also has a mystique about it, perhaps fostered by the fact that most Americans have never known anyone with a direct connection to the fighting there, coupled with the language barriers associated with the participants and the relative censorship, if not downright secrecy, concerning the Soviet side of the conflict that existed until relatively recently.

At its height in 1942, the front lines, areas of operation and territory occupied by the Axis forces along the "Eastern Front," were roughly equivalent in size to the eastern half of the entire United States, with sometimes even more extreme climatological and geographical factors added to the measure.[1] Besides the breathtaking scope and size of the land mass, the sheer numbers of men and materiel that were involved were also enormous, with a minimum of more than 5,000,000 men under arms at the start of the fighting in 1941 to a peak of around 10,000,000 in the summer of 1944.[2] The intensity of the fighting is reflected in the overall casualties: nearly 5 million military deaths among the Axis powers and a conservative estimate of more than 20 million combat and war-related deaths for the Soviets. These numbers dwarf those of the Western Allies where, for example, the United States suffered a "mere" 325,000 combat deaths in comparison. For students of military history, all types of combat were represented: high-speed mobile operations and battles of encirclement; fighting in specialized terrain such as forests, urban areas, swamps, and mountains; trench warfare and slug fests for the foot-bound and horse-supported infantry. Finally, the ideological undertones, coupled with the aforementioned intensity and brutality of the fighting, add another aspect to the conflict in

Waffen SS soldiers in winter gear.

Panzer IIIs.

the east that was largely absent in the Western Theaters of Operation. Although the efforts of the Western Allies hastened the end of the war, it was in the crucible of the Eastern Front that the war was decided and the postwar map of Europe redefined.

The war initially saw the pitting of the world's best military at the time—the German Armed Forces (*Wehrmacht*)—against a poorly led and organized Soviet military—the Red Army. The German Army was battle tested and hardened as the result of several previously highly successful campaigns, while the Red Army was suffering a crisis in leadership and organization due to bloody purges of its leadership by Stalin. In time, however, the *Wehrmacht* suffered from the constant grind of operations, the inability of German industry to sustain the force, the specter of a two-front war, and a number of other debilitating factors to lose the strategic and operational initiative

to a robust and adaptive Red Army, which eventually became its equal in the operational realm. While historians may disagree as to the exact time frame for each of the shifts in strategic dominance, the Soviet model for judging the "Great Patriotic War"[3] works well:

- **Phase 1—German strategic dominance:** From the start of operations in the East (22 June 1941) to the end of German offensive actions in the effort to take Stalingrad (18 November 1942)

- **Phase 2—Transitional period for strategic dominance:** From the start of the Soviet counteroffensive at Stalingrad (19 November 1942) to the breaching of German defenses along the Dniepr and the subsequent advances into Belorussia and the Ukraine (roughly December 1943)

- **Phase 3—Soviet strategic dominance:** From December 1943 until the defeat of Germany in May 1945.[4]

GERMAN DOMINANCE

Feeling confident in the abilities of his armed forces after a string of unprecedented victories, Hitler formally announced his intent to invade the Soviet Union in December 1940 with a planning date of May 1941 for the start of Operation Barbarossa, the code name for the offensive. In doing so, he violated his own principles in not allowing Germany to be involved in a two-front war. Nevertheless, he sensed weakness on the part of the Western Allies and perceived no immediate threat emanating from there. He also felt that the Soviet Union would topple like a house of cards and he could take a calculated risk, even though the two socialist powers had signed a non-aggression treaty, which had been scrupulously upheld by the Soviets. For Hitler, it was intended to be a campaign that would cause the world to "hold its breath."

After a delay at least partially caused by the fighting in the Balkans,[5] the attack order was given for 22 June 1941. Massed along the Soviet-occupied Polish zone and the frontiers of the Soviet Union was the largest concentration of forces the world had ever seen, including

Events before Barbarossa

May–Sept 1939	Soviet Union fights Japan at Khalkhyn Gol
Aug 23, 1939	Nazi–Soviet Pact signed
Sept 1, 1939	Germany invades Poland
Sept 17, 1939	Soviet Union invades Poland
Oct 1939	Germans establish first Jewish ghetto in Poland
Nov 30, 1939	Soviet Union invades Finland (Winter War)
April 9, 1940	Germany invades Norway, Denmark
April–May 1940	Soviets execute more than 20,000 Poles in Katyn Massacre
May 10, 1940	Germany invades France, Belgium, the Netherlands, Luxembourg
June 1940	Soviet Union invades Lithuania, Estonia, Latvia
July 10, 1940	Germany begins Battle of Britain
Sept 27, 1940	Tripartite Pact signed by Germany, Italy, Japan
April 6, 1941	Germany invades Yugoslavia, Greece
April 13, 1941	Soviet–Japanese Neutrality Pact signed
June 22, 1941	Germany invades Soviet Union

virtually all of the armored formations of the German Army and the *SS-Verfügungstruppe.*[6] In round numbers, the German forces totaled approximately 3,050,000 men in 207 infantry divisions, of which 13 were motorized, and three brigades. In addition, there were 3,350 armored fighting vehicles of all types, mostly concentrated in the 17 armored (*Panzer*) divisions. The German Air Force (*Luftwaffe*) supported the ground operations with approximately 4,000 aircraft, to include liaison and transport assets, but only 3,000 of its aircraft were reported as being operational. The ground forces were assigned to three field-army groups, North, Center, and South, which had general geographic objectives of Leningrad, Moscow, and the fertile farmlands of the Ukraine.

Facing the Germans and their allies were 3,000,000 Soviet troops in the front line with another 1,000,000 in reserve. In terms of armor, the Germans faced some

German infantry on the march.

22,500 tanks and almost 5,000 armored cars, more than twice armor strategist and tactician General Heinz Guderians's pre-war estimate of 10,000, which was considered a substantial exaggeration at the time. Impressive though these figures were, only 970 of the vehicles were the revolutionary T-34 medium tank, armed with a 76.2mm main gun, which far outclassed anything the Germans then fielded.[7]

The war against the Soviet Union will be such that it cannot be conducted in a knightly fashion. The struggle is one of ideologies and racial differences and will have to be conducted with unprecedented, unmerciful, and unrelenting harshness."

➢ *Hitler, March 1941*

German soldiers pose with a Soviet flag.

The idea was to conduct a war of maneuver along the entire front, with the focal point (*Schwerpunkt*) of the offensive in the center under the overall command of Army Group Center (*Heeresgruppe Mitte*). Germany's forces were able to make significant gains from the onset of the offensive, partly due to the ill-advised forward positioning of the majority of the Red Army's combat forces, a move that has caused some historians to question whether Stalin was planning his own attack against Germany and her allies.[8] Regardless, that disposition of forces, coupled with the virtually complete surprise that

was achieved when the attack was launched, the destruction of much of the Red Air Force's tactical fleet on the ground, and the slow and inept response starting with the commanders in the field and moving up the chain-of-command, led to unprecedented ground gains and a relatively quick breaching of the frontier defenses and then the Stalin Line.

Unlike the French campaign, where there was a clear strategic objective to drive to the Channel and isolate the French and British armies in Belgium, the field army groups were sent in three directions with the overall strategic goal

being contentious, with one camp arguing for the elimination of the Soviet forces in the field and the other camp arguing for decapitating the leadership centers of the Soviet Union, primarily Leningrad and Moscow. As a result of the main effort eventually being focused on destroying the Red Army, particularly since the drive in the south was being slowed considerably by stubborn Soviet resistance, the drive on Moscow was delayed by more than a month.

Forces were diverted to contain and eliminate huge pockets of Soviet forces through the use of gigantic pincers movements conducted by Army Groups Center and South. At Kiev, four Soviet field armies and parts of a fifth—some forty-three divisions—were trapped. The Germans claimed 652,000 prisoners and the Soviets themselves admitted to 616,000 casualties.

Contrary to the myth of blitzkrieg and its mechanized juggernaut, the German war machine relied on horses until the end of the war.

However, valuable time was lost, allowing the Soviet forces to reconstitute with astonishing rapidity. On the German side, casualties continued to mount and, by late August, the Eastern Front was short 200,000 troops and most panzer divisions were down to 20%–30% of their initial tank strength.

The diversions of the summer deprived the Germans of the opportunity to take Moscow before the onset of winter weather, which proved to be the unhinging of the campaign in 1941. In early October, the autumn rains commenced—the start of the soon-to-be-dreaded *Rasputitsa* mud season—turning the already terrible roads into almost impassable quagmires that were difficult to negotiate even by tracked vehicles. The already inadequate German motor transport, consisting of far too many types, including a significant number of captured vehicles, could not cope with the conditions. Supplies to the attacking divisions were severely curtailed, with less than half of the required tonnage being delivered.

The Red Army and Navy and the whole Soviet people must fight for every inch of Soviet soil, fight to the last drop of blood for our towns and villages."

➤ *Stalin, June 1941*

Funneling in fresh reserves from the East,[9] Stalin was able to launch a counteroffensive that sent the Germans reeling for the first time and almost led to the destruction of a major portion of the German Army.[10] It would be able to recover and establish a winter defensive line, but its "nimbus of invincibility" had been shattered, with corresponding negative effects on German morale.

Above: Waffen SS soldiers wearing their distinctive camouflage.
Right: German infantrymen prepared for action.

GERMAN DOMINANCE

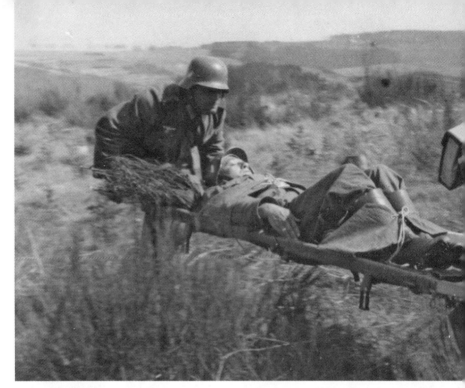

Soldiers pause from the march.

The Russian colossus has been underestimated."

> *Gen. Franz Halder, August 1941*

Evacuating the wounded.

Soviet prisoners being driven before a German Panzer II tank.

GERMAN DOMINANCE

The most important goal of the campaign against the Jewish–Bolshevik system is the complete smashing of its means of power. . . . The soldier must have complete understanding of the necessity of the severe but justified atonement of Jewish subhumanity."

> ➣ *Field Marshal Walter von Reichenau,*
> *October 1941*

Above: A Panzer IV tank.

Left: German Hiwis. Germans relied on these captured "volunteers" for rear-area responsibilities.

GERMAN DOMINANCE

Wilhelm Ritter von Leeb Career Highlights

Leeb commanded Army Group North during Operation Barbarossa.

1876	Born in Bavaria
c. 1900	Serves in Boxer Rebellion
1914–18	Serves on Eastern Front of World War I
1938	Commands 12th Army, participates in occupation of Sudetenland
1940	Commands Army Group C in France
1941	Operation Barbarossa, begins siege of Leningrad
Jan 1942	Relieved of command
1948	Sentenced to time served at Nuremberg
1956	Dies of heart attack

Left: A howitzer being fired.
Above, below: German artillery in action.

Fedor von Bock Career Highlights

Bock commanded Army Group Center during Operation Barbarossa.

1880	Born in Prussia
1914–18	Battalion commander in World War I
1935	Made commander of Third Army Group
1938	Leads military in Anschluss in Austria, invasion of Czechoslovakia
Sept 1939	Leads Army Group North in Poland
April–June 1940	Leads Army Group B in invasion of Low Countries and France
July 1940	Promoted to field marshal
June 1941	Operation Barbarossa begins
Oct 1941–Jan 1942	Operation Typhoon against Moscow
Jan 1942	Leads Army Group South
July 1942	Relieved of command
May 1945	Killed after air attack on his car

A German armored personnel carrier in a burning village.

A view of another Sd.Kfz.251, the standard German halftrack of World War II.

Soldiers bundled up against the Russian winter.

"Russia is like a cold iron coffin."

> ➤ *German soldier*

Although the German military had entered the conflict with some trepidation, based on the enemy's order of battle and the vastness of the terrain, it initially applied the same formula it had used in the past with unprecedented success in the West. This worked well during the initial weeks of campaigning, when the German's martial reputation preceded it, but problems soon began to surface that would haunt the Germans for the rest of the war in the East. While not complete, this listing addresses the major tactical issues that confronted the German armed forces on the ground:

- The topography of the Soviet Union varied widely, with vast tracts of forested terrain in the north proving to be essentially unsuitable for armored operations, while the harsh climate and vast distances of the steppes in the south induced accelerated wear and tear of combat and tactical vehicles of all types. While the center section of the Eastern Front had terrain features similar to continental Europe, it had waterways approximately every 25 kilometers that could not be crossed without existing suitable infrastructure or engineer assistance, coupled with vast tracts of forested terrain and marshland.

- The transportation infrastructure was completely inadequate for fielding a modern army. Not only did the railways in Soviet

In the early phases of Barbarossa, in the marshes of western Russian and Ukraine, insects were a constant bother. These soldiers are wearing anti-mosquito netting.

countries use a different gauge than the European system, which necessitated a conversion of track in order to transport supplies, logistical support, and reinforcements to the front by train, their capacity was limited by long stretches of single rail. More importantly, from a tactical perspective, was the complete inadequacy of the road network, with only a few roads corresponding to the common "improved" road of Western Europe. Most were of hard-packed dirt or gravel construction that quickly turned into dust bowls after even the first combat elements passed. Whenever it rained, they turned into virtual rivers of mud. Likewise, bridges usually did not have the carrying capacity for most heavy military vehicles, having been constructed for light farm traffic. The further either side got from its logistical support base, the more difficulty it had in supporting its forces in the field.

- While the average Soviet soldier was initially poorly led and showed little to no initiative, he

Gerd von Rundstedt Career Highlights

Rundstedt commanded Army Group South during Operation Barbarossa.

1875	Born in Germany
1914–18	Chief of staff positions during World War I
1938	Army commander during Sudetenland crisis
	Retires
1939	Commander, Army Group South in Poland
1940	Commander, Army Group A in France
	Promoted to field marshal
	Plans aborted Operation Sealion
	Commander-in-Chief West
1941	Commander, Army Group South (Barbarossa)
	Dismissed but reinstated by Hitler after withdrawal from Rostov
1942–July 1944	Commander-in-Chief West (D-Day, Normandy)
1944	Heads Court of Honor after July 20 plot against Hitler
Sept 1944–1945	Commander-in-Chief West (Siegfried Line, Ardennes, Rhine)
1945	Captured by Allies, accused of war crimes, never tried
1945–49	Imprisoned
1953	Dies in Germany

was stoic and stubborn in the defense and willing to lay down his life in even hopeless situations. This was a new experience for the German soldier, who had been accustomed to foes who either surrendered with little or no fight or at least knew when there was no use in carrying on a struggle. He also adapted well to life in the field, willing to forego creature comforts and endure hardships that were unfathomable to the average German soldier. The German forces were also woefully unprepared for the harshness of the Russian winter, with the first one in 1941–42 being the most severe in more than half a century. Subsequent winters were milder and the Germans learned to adapt, but winter campaigning always imposed a tremendous strain on the system and personnel.

I am broken in every fiber."

> *German soldier*

- The vast quantities of men and materiel available to the Soviets also came as a shock to German forces in the field. They seemed to have inexhaustible supplies of men, whom they were also willing to commit no matter the cost. While many of the armored vehicles initially employed were inferior to those of the Germans, their sheer numbers proved daunting, even if they were poorly led, committed piecemeal, and had hardly any radio capabilities. The introduction of vastly superior tanks that summer—the vaunted T-34 and the KV series of vehicles, which could scarcely be countered by German weaponry then fielded—were a serious

"Fight to the Last"

On 16 August 1941, Stalin issued Order No. 270, which ordered that deserting commanders be shot, that encircled units "fight to the last," and that surrendering soldiers would be "destroyed" as traitors and their families denied benefits.

Not only our friends, but also our enemies are forced to acknowledge that, in our war of liberation from German–Fascist invaders, that elements of the Red Army, the vast majority of them, their commanders and commissars conduct themselves with good behavior, courageously, and sometimes—outright heroically. Even those parts of our army who, by circumstances are detached from the army and encircled, preserve the spirit of resistance and courage, not surrendering, trying to cause more damage to the enemy and to leave the encirclement. It is known that such parts of our army continue to attack the enemy, and take every opportunity to defeat the enemy and break out of their encirclement. . . .

Can we put up with in the Red Army cowards, deserters who surrender themselves to the enemy as prisoners or their craven superiors, who at the first hitch on the front tear off their insignia and desert to the rear? No we cannot! If we unleash these cowards and deserters they, in a very short time, will destroy our country. Cowards and deserters must be destroyed. ∎

The Soviet T-34, the backbone of the Soviet war machine.

detriment to morale. While the constant upgrading of the main German medium tank, the Panzer IV, ensured rough one-on-one combat parity for the rest of the war and the introduction of the Panther medium and Tiger heavy tanks enabled local superiority on occasion, the smaller German industrial output, coupled with the diversion of assets to other fronts, meant that the Germans were always mounting a reactive effort from 1943 on.

Right: A downed Soviet SB-2.

The German Stuka, the famous air component of the blitzkrieg.

The Heinkel 111, one of the mainstay bombers of the German *Luftwaffe*.

AftER SUFFERING ITS FIRST operational setback in the winter of 1941–42, the German armed forces had to regroup and rebuild. The Eastern Front remained essentially static for the first half of 1942, except for local operations designed to streamline and improve defensive positions. Unable to conduct a major push along the entire front, the high command eventually opted for its main offensive in the south, while *Heeresgruppe Nord* was to take Leningrad and link up with Finnish forces and *Heeresgruppe Mitte* was to conduct containment operations. To this end, large amounts of armored and motorized forces were transferred to *Heeresgruppe Süd* and many

1942 on the Eastern Front

Jan 8–Apr 20	Soviet Rzhev–Vyazma operation
May 12–28	Second Battle of Kharkov
June 28–July 24	Battle of Voronezh
June 28–Nov 24	Case Blue (Caucasus)
July 4	Sevastopol falls to Germans
Aug 23–Feb 2, 1943	Battle of Stalingrad
Nov 19–23	Operation Uranus (Stalingrad)
Nov 25–Dec 20	Operation Mars (Rzhev)
Dec 12–Feb 18, 1943	Operation Saturn (Caucasus)

A common sight on the Eastern Front: Soviet villages and vestiges of the Russian Orthodox church.

formations that remained in the center and the north were forced to detach major elements to augment the new *Schwerpunkt*.[11]

The overall plan in the south—Code "Blue" (*Fall Blau*)—had a twofold objective, for which two field-army groups were eventually formed. *Heeresgruppe A* was tasked with crossing the Caucasus and reaching the strategically important oil fields around Baku. *Heeresgruppe B* was assigned the mission of covering the flanks of its southern neighbor while advancing toward the Volga and Stalingrad. This, in effect, created two competing *Schwerpunkte* that operated simultaneously instead of conducting a coordinated and multiphased

Aleksandr Vasilevsky Career Highlights

1895	Born in Russia
1915–17	Serves in World War I as company and battalion commander
1919–20	Participates in Polish–Soviet War
1921	Fights against Whites in Russian Civil War
1937	Appointed to General Staff
1938	Made member of Communist Party
1939	Plans Winter War against Finland
1941	Deputy Chief of the General Staff during Operation Barbarossa
	Involved in defense of Moscow
1942	Acting Chief of Staff
	Second Battle of Kharkov
	Leningrad
	Chief of Staff / Deputy Minister of Defense
1942–43	Stalingrad
1943	General of the Army / Marshal of the Soviet Union
	Battle of Kursk
1944	Dnieper offensive
	Wounded when car hits mine
	Operation Bagration
	Hero of the Soviet Union
1945	East Prussian Operation
	Commander-in-Chief in Far East
	Invasion of Manchuria
	Hero of the Soviet Union (2nd award)
1949–53	Defense Minister under Stalin
1957	Eased out of power by Khrushchev
1977	Dies

effort. Spectacular land gains were made in the direction of the oil fields, but continuing logistical problems for the German forces meant that the offensive eventually sputtered to a slow crawl. Moreover, the Soviet forces fell back in relatively good order, thus ensuring that there were no major battles of encirclement, such as had occurred the previous year.

It is necessary to use special energy to beat the enemy in Kaluga, to break him into little pieces, to make no concessions at all, and to give the enemy no quarter."

> ➤ *Marshal Zhukov,*
> *December 1941*

A German 88mm battery.

Not One Step Back!

On 28 July 1941, Stalin issued Order No. 227:

The enemy sends new forces to the front without regard to heavy losses and penetrates deep into the Soviet Union, seizing new regions, destroying our cities and villages, and violating, plundering, and killing our population. The German invaders penetrate toward Stalingrad, to the Volga, and want at any cost to trap Kuban and the Northern Caucasus, with their oil and grain. Part of the troops of the Southern Front, following the panic-mongers, have left Rostov and Novocherkassk without severe resistance and without orders from Moscow, covering their banners with shame....

Some stupid people at the front calm themselves with talk that we can retreat further to the east, as we have a lot of territory, a lot of ground, a lot of population, and that there will always be plentiful bread for us. They want to justify the notorious behavior at the front. But such talk is falsehood, helpful only to our enemies.

Each commander, Red Army soldier and political commissar should understand that our means are not limitless. The territory of the Soviet state is not a desert, but people—workers, peasants, intelligentsia, our fathers, mothers, wives, brothers, children. The territory of the Soviet Union which the enemy has captured and aims to capture means bread and other products for the army, metal and fuel for industry, factories, plants supplying the army with arms and ammunition, railroads....

It is necessary to eliminate talk that we can retreat endlessly, that we have vast territory, that our country is great and rich, that there is a large population, and that bread always will be abundant. Such talk is false and parasitic; it weakens us and aids the enemy....

It is time to finish retreating. Not one step back! ∎

To the north, *Heeresgruppe B* also found rough going, and its exhausted forces were unable to take the city of Stalingrad, despite controlling some 90% of the metropolis at one point. The *6. Armee*, which was invested with the capture of the city, was overextended and relied on various Axis allies to protect the flanks. In the end, the Soviets launched counteroffensives that broke through

Semyon Timoshenko Career Highlights

1895	Born in Ukraine
1914–17	Cavalryman in World War I
1918–21	Joins Bolsheviks, serves in Russian Civil War
1930s	Commander in Belorussia, Kiev, Caucasus, Kharkov, Ukraine
1939–40	Commands Soviet forces in Winter War
1941	Chairman of Soviet Armed Forces High Command (Stavka)
	Sent to oversee retreat to Smolensk
	Rostov counteroffensives
1942	Second Battle of Kharkov
	Stalingrad
1943	Leningrad
1944	Caucasus, Baltic
1970	Dies

German soldiers smugly demonstrate their "superiority" over Soviet peasants.

the flank protection, encircled the forces in Stalingrad, and sealed their fate. This also forced the precipitous retreat of the forces of *Heeresgruppe A* in a difficult but ultimately successful effort to avoid encirclement and suffer the same fate as sister formations to the north. It was largely thanks to the Soviets' overestimation of their capabilities that the Germans were eventually able to stop their offensive efforts, most notably at Kharkov, and reestablish some semblance of a defensive front, enabling them to plan another operational offensive for 1943. Total disaster had been prevented, as it had also been in the winter of 1941–42, but the loss at Stalingrad was an operational catastrophe of the first magnitude.

German infantry digging in.

B **oys, this is the end for me, but you go on fighting."**

> ➤ *Lt. Gen. Mikhail Yefremov, April 1942*

With the German failure to capture Stalingrad, the strategic imperative began to shift slowly but inexorably to the Soviets. German losses and those of the Italian, Hungarian, and Rumanian forces could not be replaced. Tanks, aircraft, trucks, and other vital military items were also pouring into the Soviet Union, mainly from the United States, as a result of the Lend-Lease Program, allowing Soviet factories to concentrate on artillery, aircraft, and tanks.[12]

STRATEGIC DOMINANCE IN THE BALANCE

The Soviet winter offensive of 1942–43 was just as ambitious as that of 1941–42. It intended to knock Germany out of the war or at least recover the Ukraine and, in the process, inflict crippling casualties. Had all of *Heeresgruppe A* been trapped in the Caucasus, it would have been a disaster far greater than Stalingrad, but the *1. Panzer-Armee* managed to escape the trap, with the remainder of the field army group being trapped on the Taman Peninsula, where it resisted Soviet assaults until October 1943, before being evacuated by sea.

Despite the serious setbacks, the Germans demonstrated that they were still the masters of maneuver warfare when they thwarted two Soviet operations, named Gallup (29 January) and Star (2 February), which were intended to exploit the 600-kilometer gap between the depleted *2. Armee* to the North and the *4. Panzer-Armee* in the South. *Generalfeldmarschall* Erich von Manstein, considered Germany's foremost operational commander, commanded *Heeresgruppe Don*[13] and was tasked with restoring a sound defensive line in that sector around Kharkov.

Victory at Stalingrad

On 25 January 1943, Stalin congratulated the Red Army:

As a result of two months of offensive engagements, the Red Army has broken through the defenses of the German–fascist troops on a wide front, routed 102 enemy divisions, captured over 200,000 prisoners, 13,000 guns and a large quantity of their war material, and advanced about 400 kilometers. Our troops have won an important victory. The offensive of our troops continues.

I congratulate the Red Army men, commanders and political workers of the South–Western, Southern, Don, North Caucasian, Voronezh, Kalinin, Volkhov and Leningrad fronts on their victory over the German–fascist invaders and their allies—the Romanians, Italians and Hungarians—at Stalingrad, on the Don, in the North Caucasus, at Voronezh, in the Velikie Luki area and south of Lake Ladoga.

I thank the Command and the glorious troops who have routed the Hitlerite armies at the approaches to Stalingrad, who have broken the blockade of Leningrad and liberated from the German invaders the towns of Kantemirovka, Belovodsk, Morozovsky, Millerovo, Starobelsk, Kotelnikovo, Zimovniki, Elista, Salsk, Mozdok, Nalchik, Mineralniye Vody, Pyatigorsk, Stavropol, Armavir, Valuiki, Rossosh, Ostrogozhsk, Velikie Luki, Schluesselburg, Voronezh and many other towns and thousands of populated places.

Forward to the rout of the German invaders and their expulsion from the boundaries of our Motherland! ∎

The city was to be defended by the powerful and newly formed *II. SS-Panzer-Korps,* consisting of *SS-Panzergrenadier-Division "Leibstandarte Adolf Hitler," SS-Panzergrenadier-Division "Das Reich,"* and *SS-Panzergrenadier-Division "Totenkopf,"* with each of these divisions having a company of the formidable Tiger I heavy tank.[14]

SS-Obergruppenführer[15] Paul Hausser, the Commanding General of the *SS* corps, ordered a withdrawal from the city on 16 February, in contravention of Hitler's orders. It was almost surrounded, and Hausser feared his forces would be completely cut off and destroyed. Moreover, it appeared to the Germans that the Soviets

STRATEGIC DOMINANCE IN THE BALANCE

Another view of the Soviet T-34.

were reaching the culminating point of their offensives. Manstein intended to use his two armored corps, the *II. SS-Panzer-Korps* and the *XXXXVIII. Panzer-Korps*, to eliminate the Soviet spearhead and drive the advancing forces back to the River Donets, whereupon his forces would attack to the north and recapture Kharkov. Manstein's counteroffensive began on 20 February. With the Tigers dominating the battlefield and the Panzer IVs able to destroy the T-34s at long range, three Soviet tank corps were destroyed in a matter of days. Soviet counterattacks were brushed aside with comparative ease as the Germans totally outmaneuvered the Soviet units.

I shot the commander and commissar of one regiment, and a short while later, I shot two brigade commanders and their commissars. This caught everyone off guard. We made sure news of this got to the men."

> *General Vasily Chuikov, on his arrival at Stalingrad*

SS-Panzergrenadier-Division "Totenkopf" cut the last lines of communication for the Soviet forces in Kharkov on 13 March, and the city was retaken the next day. Manstein's offensive operations recommenced on 15 March, with the *II. SS-Panzer-Korps* as its spearhead. The Soviet 3rd Tank Army was thrown back across the Donets, and the loss of Belgorod on 18 March severed the escape route of the 69th Army, which tried and failed to make a large-scale breakout over the next four days. The spring thaw ended the fighting, with the Germans not only once again escaping total destruction but also inflicting significant casualties on their opponents. The German position in the Ukraine was still strong and another offensive in the

A German supply depot.

summer was a threat that could not be ignored.

Once again, German rapid responsiveness to changing situations, superb staff work, and effective tactical command and control proved superior to their Soviet counterparts. They were able to fight well with limited resources, but their actions were increasingly becoming reactive rather than proactive. The Soviets seemed to learn rapidly from their mistakes, especially at the operational and strategic levels.

The German summer offensive of 1943, unlike the first two, had strictly limited aims. It intended to pinch off the huge salient of Soviet forces in the center of the Eastern Front around the Kursk area. The Germans intended to cause as many

1943 on the Eastern Front	
Feb 2	Final German surrender at Stalingrad
Feb 8–16	Soviets take Kursk, Rostov, Kharkov
Feb 19–March 15	Third Battle of Kharkov
July 5–Aug 23	Battle of Kursk
Aug 3–23	Fourth Battle of Kharkov
Aug 26–Dec 23	Battle of the Dnieper
Nov 3–Dec 22	Second Battle of Kiev

The Germans relied heavily on literal horsepower to move their army across Europe and Asia.

casualties as possible to forestall any Soviet offensive. In the face of a resurgent Red Army and with the threat of an Allied invasion in the West, the best the Germans could hope for was a stalemate in the East and a negotiated settlement.

Operation Citadel has been covered in such detail that only the briefest summary is necessary. In essence, it was an unimaginative assault with two pincer arms directed against obvious objectives at the northern and southern base of the Soviet salient. It was conducted with 770,000 troops and 2,450 tanks and assault guns and supported by 7,400 guns and mortars. The Soviets, for their part, correctly anticipated the objectives of the German attack and fortified accordingly, establishing successive

These panzers have been camouflaged for winter.

defensive belts, which were manned by 1,900,000 men and more than 5,000 tanks and self-propelled guns. These were supported by more than 30,000 guns and mortars. Operation Citadel might have worked in April, as originally proposed and when the Soviets had not yet fortified the salient, but by 5 July it was an offensive that no one in the German high command, from Hitler down, really wanted. Nonetheless, it continued under the weight of its own inertia, since it seemed nothing better could be proposed.

Why do we want to attack in the East at all this year?"

> *General Heinz Guderian, before the Battle of Kursk*

One of the reasons for the perhaps fateful delay was the desire to reconstitute the badly mauled panzer forces under the tutelage of its new commander, *Generaloberst* Guderian, who had been reinstated on active duty after his relief by Hitler in December 1941. Guderian used the short time available

Heinz Guderian Career Highlights

1888	Born in West Prussia
1907	Entered army
1914–18	World War I
1919	Selected to serve in Reichswehr
1927	Transferred to transport and motorized tactics
1931	Chief of Staff, inspectorate of motorized troops
1935	Commander, 2nd Panzer Division
1937	*Achtung–Panzer!* published
1938	Commander, XVI Army Corps
1939	Commander, XIX Corps in Poland
1940	Invasion of France
1941	Commander, 2nd Panzer Group/Army (Barbarossa)
Dec 1941	Relieved of command
1943	Inspector General of Armored Troops
1944	Chief of Staff of the Army
1945–48	Prisoner of Allies, no charges brought
1954	Dies

to rebuild formations, both with equipment and leadership. In the same period, new armored fighting vehicles were being introduced, including the new Panzer V "Panther" medium tank, and existing designs continued to be upgraded, generally with more powerful main guns. High expectations were placed on the Panther, with about 160 available on 6 July. Far from being a decisive factor in the battle, the Panther suffered from a variety of teething troubles, with several catching fire and burning out on the way to the battlefield. By 10 July, about twenty had been destroyed by enemy action, compared to some eighty in short- and long-term repair. It has been claimed that the Panthers destroyed some 270 Soviet tanks—some at ranges of 3,000 meters—but it was a classic example of too little and too late. The Panther was to develop into one of the outstanding tanks of the war, but its battlefield debut was less than auspicious.[16]

Above: A German ambulance crew.
Below: A German motorcycle crew.

A German artilleryman.

A German battery of 88mm guns.

The Russians are not men, but some kind of cast-iron creatures."

> ➤ *German soldier at Stalingrad*

In the North, *Generaloberst* Model's 9. *Armee* had only progressed 13 kilometers by 10 July, four days after the start of the offensive. In the same period, *Generaloberst* Hoth's 4. *Panzer-Armee* advanced 32 kilometers in the south. The engagement of Prokhorovka on 12 July has often been incorrectly called the largest tank battle of the war, involving thousands of tanks.[17] The reality is less dramatic: The

III. *Panzer-Korps* and the II. SS-*Panzer-Korps* fielded approximately 470 tanks and assault guns against some 870 tanks and assault guns of the 5th Guards Tank Army. German losses for the engagement can be estimated as a fairly modest fifty-four tanks and assault guns compared to 334 Soviet tanks and assault guns. Certainly, there was no breakthrough at Prokhorovka, but there was no shattering German defeat either. Nonetheless, the Germans suffered losses that were irreplaceable; for the Soviets, the losses were barely noticeable.[18]

Loading an artillery piece.

Above : German soldiers in defensive positions.
Below: On the march in Russia.

Above: Thawing snow could turn roads into a muddy morass that slowed the German offensive.

Right: A German Panzer IV, whitewashed for winter operations.

A Soviet KV-2 tank, captured by the Germans.

Every German must be made to feel that he is living under the muzzle of a Russian gun."

> *General Vasily Chuikov, at Stalingrad*

The Germans called off the offensive for several reasons, to include having to withdraw forces to contend with the Allied invasion of Sicily, but the more compelling reason was the launching of Soviet counteroffensives, which skillfully played off the stalemating of the German effort. In the north, Orel was recaptured on 6 August. A southern operation commenced on 3 August, with Belgorod liberated three days later and Kharkov recaptured for the last time on 23 August.

STRATEGIC DOMINANCE IN THE BALANCE

A German radio team.

The battle to crush Hitler's so-called "Eastern Rampart," which ran along the Dnieper River, was one of the largest fought on the Eastern Front and of enormous magnitude. The Soviet intention was to liberate the Ukraine, recover the vital Donbass industrial region, and retake Kiev. To accomplish these objectives, they assembled five Fronts (field army groups) consisting of thirty field armies, each comprising between two and five rifle, tank, or mechanized corps, plus attached elements such as tank and artillery brigades. These ground forces were supported by five air armies. The forces totaled 2,600,000 men, 51,000 guns and mortars, 2,400 tanks and assault guns, and 2,100 combat aircraft.

The opposing German forces comprised the *2. Armee* from *Heeresgruppe Mitte*, which was commanded by *Generalfeldmarschall* von Kluge, and the *4. Panzer-Armee* and three field armies[19]—the 1st, 6th, and 8th—of *Heeresgruppe Süd*, commanded by the brilliant tactician, *Generalfeldmarschall* von Manstein. In all, the Germans fielded 1,240,000 men, 12,600 guns and mortars, and around 2,000 tanks and assault guns. In terms of combat strength, only approximately 700 tanks and 400 assault guns were actually

operational on the whole of the Eastern Front. *Luftflotte 4* provided air support, but fewer than 300 aircraft were operational out of the 600 it had in its inventory.

People have no idea what's going on here. Not a single promise is kept."

> *German soldier at Stalingrad*

The Germans were surprised by both the speed of the advance and the skillful use of mobile groups that kept them off balance. By 25 September, major Soviet bridgeheads had been established at Rzhishchev and Veliki Burkin, in advance of Manstein's mechanized formations. In all, twenty-three bridgeheads were eventually established across the Dnieper. The large Burkin Bridgehead was soon cordoned off by ten German divisions, however, and the remaining bridgeheads were placed under continuous fire. Soviet general Vatutin's breakout attempts cost the Red Army considerable tank and infantry casualties. Conversely, the German forces were not strong enough to eliminate these bridgeheads, despite considerable reinforcements from the West, including substantial numbers of Tigers and Panthers, with all attempts ending with irreplaceable

STRATEGIC DOMINANCE IN THE BALANCE

Erich von Manstein Career Highlights

1887	Born in Prussian aristocracy
1906	Commissioned, Third Foot Guards Regiment
1907	Promoted to lieutenant
1913–14	Officer training program, Prussian War Academy
1914–18	World War I (invasion of Belgium, Namur, Masurian Lakes, Verdun, Somme, Hindenburg Line, Riga)
1919	Selected for service in Reichswehr
1921	Company commander in 5th Prussian Infantry Regiment
1927	General Staff in Berlin
1934	Chief of Staff, Wehrkreiskommando III
1935	Head of operations, Army General Staff
1936	Deputy chief of staff, General Beck
1938	Commander, 18th Infantry Division
April 1939	Speaks at Hitler's 50th birthday
Aug 1939	Chief of Staff, Army Group South in Poland
1939–40	Plans invasion of France
1940	Commander, XXXVIII Army Corps (Battle of France)
1941	Commander, LVI Panzer Corps (Barbarossa)
Sept 1941	Commander, 11th Army in Crimea/Sevastopol
Aug 1942	Transferred to Leningrad
1942–43	Commander, Army Group Don in Stalingrad
Oct 1942	Son killed in war
Feb 1943–Apr 1944	Commander, Army Group South (Kursk, Belgorod–Kharkov, Dnieper)
1949	Found guilty of nine charges, including permitting deportation and execution of civilians, and sentenced to 18 years
1953	Released from prison, thanks to Winston Churchill and Konrad Adenauer
1955	Memoir *Verlorene Siege* published
1973	Dies

losses in tanks and infantry. The Panthers were still proving to be prone to numerous mechanical breakdowns, thereby nullifying their role in establishing armored supremacy over the now inadequately armed and armored T-34s.

On 15 October, there was a major breakout from the Myshuryn Rog Bridgehead. The Germans had been focusing on the Burkin Lodgment. Soviet operational prowess was essentially the equal of the Germans at this point, with the student in some cases now becoming the teacher. A major counteroffensive by the new Commanding General of the *XXXX. Panzer-Korps, Generalleutnant* Ferdinand Schörner, who

had no experience in the Ukraine or of large-scale armored operations, was mounted near Krivoi Rog from 28–31 October. The German forces included six panzer divisions, three *Panzergrenadier* divisions, and *schwere Panzer-Abteilung 506*, a heavy tank battalion equipped with the Tiger I. Schörner largely bungled the operation, much to the chagrin of Manstein, by starting the attack before all his tanks had arrived and attacking the salient frontally instead of mounting a pincer operation against the base. The attack did, however, seal a serious breach in the German front, but this respite was only temporary.

Left: The feared Soviet Katyusha rocket launcher, otherwise known as "Stalin's organ."

Below: German soldiers inspect a cache of Red Army weapons.

"Here begins the ass of the world": German soldiers reflect on conditions in the East.

The German Army relied heavily on horses, contrary to popular myth.

Dead men are no longer interested in military history."

> *Field Marshal Milch,*
> *at Stalingrad*

As was increasingly the case, Hitler demanded that his battered and outnumbered formations hold their positions along the thinly manned front, even to the extent of ordering the *IV.* and *XXIX. Armee-Korps* with their eight divisions to maintain the Nikopol Bridgehead on the east bank of the Dniepr in order to protect the manganese mines on the west bank. The Soviet bridgeheads could only be contained for so long and, on 3 November, a major breakout from the Lyutezh Bridgehead was made with substantial tank and mechanized formations, including Rybalko's 3rd Guards Tank Army. For once, the Germans reacted slowly to this threat, and the speed and proficiency of the advance caught them by surprise. By 6 November, Kiev had been liberated and on 7 November the critical rail junction at Fastov was captured. On the 13th of the same month, the equally crucial rail junction at Zhitomir was taken, seriously disrupting German reinforcements from the West and causing a crisis for *Heeresgruppe Süd.*

A counterattack by the *XXXX-VIII. Panzer-Korps* recaptured Zhitomir on 20 November, causing heavy Soviet casualties, particularly Rybalko's armor, and averting a serious situation for *Heeresgruppe Süd*. However, there were no large-scale encirclements and disorganized retreats, as the Red Army was now experienced in reacting to and countering German attacks. In the South, the Soviet advance was slow and costly, with the Germans mounting a number of successful counterattacks. The Nikopol Bridgehead, defended by nine infantry divisions and the *24. Panzer-Division*, continuing to hold out against no less than four Soviet field armies.

Finally, on 24 December, Vatutin's 1st Ukrainian Front attacked the *XXXXII. Armee-Korps* with overwhelming strength, and it soon started to collapse. By 29 December, there was no continuous German front, and the *4. Panzer-Armee* was effectively shattered. Konev's forces advanced 30 kilometers in five days, coming close to destroying the *8. Armee*. The situation toward the end of December was critical for *Heeresgruppe Süd*, with the Red Army resuming the offensive, almost without pause.

Soldiers, members of Germany's elite Großdeutschland formation, on the rails.

Ivan Konev Career Highlights

1897	Born in Russia
1916	Conscripted into Russian Army for World War I
1919	Joins Bolsheviks
1938	Commander, 2nd Red Banner Army
Oct 1941–Aug 1942	Commander, Kalinin Front (Moscow, Rzhev)
Feb–July 1943	Commander, North–Western Front
July 1943–May 1945	Commander, 2nd Ukrainian Front (Kursk, Belgorod, Odessa, Kiev, Korsun–Cherkassy, Ukraine, Belarus, Poland)
1946–50	Replaces Zhukov as Deputy Minister of Defense
1953	Oversees trial of Lavrenty Beria
1956–60	Commander in Chief, Armed Forces of the Warsaw Pact
1956	Leads suppression of Hungarian Revolution
1973	Dies

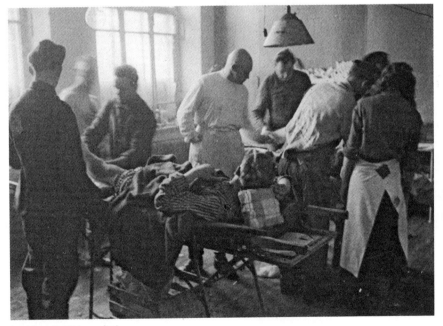

Inside a field hospital.

STRATEGIC DOMINANCE IN THE BALANCE

A battlefield meeting of German tank and infantry soldiers.

Not a single blade of grass was left standing on the darkened soil."

> *Marshal Zhukov, at Kursk*

Soviet losses were more than 1,000,000 men—including 290,000 dead or missing—and some 12,000 armored vehicles, but both personnel and equipment could be replaced, particularly as new recruits were now available from the Ukrainian populace. *Heeresgruppe Süd* suffered 370,000 casualties, with 100,000 dead or missing, and these could not be effectively

replaced.[20] German tank losses were about a fifth of the Red Army, but the Soviet Union was outproducing Germany on a massive scale, with around 20,000 tanks manufactured compared to some 6,000 German. It was also aided by Lend-Lease tanks and trucks, particularly from the United States.

What the Dniepr Campaign convincingly demonstrated was that the Red Army was now capable of mounting and, more importantly, sustaining large scale combined-arms operations simultaneously and on multiple fronts employing massive infantry, artillery,

A Soviet banner.

tank, and air superiority. The Dniepr Campaign set the basic pattern for all subsequent Soviet offensive operations: multiple attacks along an extended front, rapid reinforcement of breakthroughs, and the use of large mobile groups to disrupt and unhinge the defense, all combined with very effective tactical air support. This Soviet campaign also ushered in the 3rd Phase of the War on the Eastern Front, in which Soviet strategic dominance and victory was assured.

Towards the end of 1943 at the latest, it had become unmistakably clear that the war had been lost."

➢ *General Halder*

Victory at Kursk: The Legend Is Refuted

After the Battle of Kursk, Stalin congratulated the Red Army:

On the morning of July 5 the German–fascist troops, with large forces of tanks and infantry, supported by large air forces, passed to the offensive in the Orel–Kursk and Byelgorod–Kursk directions. The Germans hurled into attack against our troops their main forces, concentrated in the areas of Orel and Byelgorod. . . .

In fierce engagements our troops wore down and bled white the picked German divisions, and followed this up by violent counterblows by which they not only hurled back the enemy and completely restored the position they had occupied before July 5, but also broke through the enemy's defences and advanced 15 to 25 kilometers toward Orel.

The battles fought for the liquidation of the German offensive have demonstrated the high military skill of our troops. Unprecedented examples of stubbornness, steadfastness and heroism have been displayed by the men and commanders of all arms, including artillery and mortar gunners, tankmen and airmen.

Thus the German plan for a summer offensive can be considered as having failed completely. Thus the legend that in a summer offensive the Germans are always successful, and that the Soviet troops are compelled to retreat, is refuted.

I congratulate you and the troops under your command on the successful liquidation of the German summer offensive. I express my gratitude to all men, commanders and political workers of the troops under your command for their excellent operations.

Immortal glory to the heroes who fell in the fight for the freedom and honour of our Motherland! ∎

PHASE 3

SOVIET
DOMINANCE

From 24 December 1943 to early 1944, a series of operations was mounted along a 900-mile front. Designated "Right Bank Ukraine," it had the intention of destroying both *Heeresgruppe A* and *Heeresgruppe Süd*.

From 8 April to 12 May 1944 alone, there were ten separate operations— eleven if the Crimean operation is counted—employing five fronts with 2,000,000 troops, 4,000 tanks and assault guns, and 4,000 aircraft.

Hitler, as usual, interfered in the conduct of the defense with his habitual no-retreat orders, producing the inevitable disastrous effects, like the trapping of 60,000–70,000 men in the Korsun-Tscherkassy Pocket. Manstein, mindful of Stalingrad, dispatched a relief force that included eight panzer divisions to free the encircled four infantry divisions, the 5. *SS-Panzer-Division* "*Wiking*," and other formations. On 15 February, Hitler finally gave the garrison the order to break out, achieving a link up with the *III. Panzer-Korps* on 18 February. A total of 36,000 men were claimed to have broken out,[21] but at the cost of leaving all their heavy equipment behind.

"The Hour of Final Reckoning"

On 23 February 1944, Stalin issued Order No. 16:

By now it must be obvious to everyone that Hitler's Germany is irresistibly heading for catastrophe. True, conditions for the prosecution of war are more favorable for Germany in the present war than during the last World War, when from the very beginning to the end of the war she waged a struggle on two fronts. However, the great drawback for Germany is the fact that in this war the Soviet Union has proved to be much stronger than the old Tsarist Russia was in the last war.... If the Soviet Union, fighting single-handed, has not only withstood the onslaught of the German war machine, but also inflicted decisive defeats on the German-fascist troops, all the more hopeless will be the situation of Hitler's Germany when the main forces of our Allies join action, and a powerful and growing offensive of the armies of all the Allied States develops against Hitler's Germany.

The German-fascist brigands are now tossing about in search of ways to save themselves from disaster.... The fascist ringleaders make desperate attempts to provoke discord in the camp of the anti-Hitler coalition and thereby to drag out the war. Hitler's diplomats rush from one neutral country to another, striving to establish contacts with pro-Hitler elements, hinting at the possibility of a separate peace now with our State, now with our Allies. All these subterfuges of the Nazis are doomed to failure, as the anti-Hitler coalition is founded on the vital interests of the Allies who have set themselves the task of smashing Nazi Germany and her accomplices in Europe. It is this very community of basic interests that leads to the consolidation of the fighting alliance of the U.S.S.R., Britain and the U.S.A., in the progress of the war.

The hour of the final reckoning for all the crimes committed by the Nazis on Soviet soil and in the occupied countries of Europe is drawing near.... ■

A meal in the field.

More importantly, two experienced corps were effectively destroyed and played no further part in the fighting. The German relief forces suffered more than 20,000 casualties and heavy tank losses, while Soviet losses were estimated as 80,000 men and 700 tanks.

The 1st Ukrainian Front broke through to Tarnopol and Proskuroz, separating the *1. Panzer-Armee* and the *4. Panzer-Armee*, while 2nd Ukrainian Front shattered the *8. Armee*. A massive gap was created between *Heeresgruppe A* and *Heeresgruppe Süd*. The offensive continued without letup. Not even the spring thaw slowed the Red Army down, leading to a separation of the increasingly nervous German forces in Poland from those in southern Russia. By 17 April, the Soviet offensive had progressed unabated for four

months, advancing from 250 to 500 kilometers to the Polish border and the Carpathian Mountains, eliminating the entire southern sector of the German forces. From 8 April to 9 May, the Red Army retook the Crimea in an operation of stunning rapidity, shattering the *17. Armee* in the process and inflicting more than 100,000 casualties. In the North, another major operation relieved the besieged Leningrad by 20 January, the German forces being pushed back more than 150 kilometers, as far as Estonia, in some places.

Generaloberst Schörner took over command of *Heeresgruppe Südukraine*, formerly *Heeresgruppe A*, and *Generalfeldmarschall* Model now commanded *Heeresgruppe Nordukraine*. The previous

A German clears a Red Army bunker with a flamethrower.

commanders-in-chief, Kleist and Manstein, had fallen out of Hitler's favor. In the case of Manstein, the best operational-level general in the German Army was now permanently removed from command. If the situation looked remorselessly grim to the Germans in April, it was to become far worse in June.

Prussian field marshals do not mutiny."

➤ *Manstein, on the July 20 plot*

THE RED ARMY WAS NO LONGER just quantitatively superior in armor, but it was rapidly catching up in the quality of its tanks as well. The T-34/85, with its high velocity 85mm main gun housed in a redesigned 3-man turret, was intended

1944 on the Eastern Front	
Jan 27	Siege of Leningrad ends
Apr 8–May 12	Battle of the Crimea
June 22–Aug 19	Operation Bagration
July 13–Aug 29	Lvov–Sandomierz offensive
Aug 1–Oct 2	Warsaw Uprising
Sept 14–Nov 24	Soviet Baltic offensive
Dec 24– Feb 13, 1945	Siege of Budapest

to counter the Panther, now considered its most dangerous opponent at the front. A tank battalion in mid-1944 consisted of twenty-one T-34/85s, three of these battalions forming the principal striking force of a tank brigade. Although the new T-34 was not quite a match for the Panther, it was markedly superior to the latest upgrade to the Panzer IV, the *Ausführung J*.

Also appearing at this time was the formidable IS-2 "Stalin," with its heavy armor and massive 122mm D-25T main gun. The IS-2 gave both the Tiger I and the Panther plenty of headaches, as it was capable of destroying either vehicle at normal combat ranges of 1,000 meters. However, both German tanks could also knock out the Stalin at that range, and their superior optics gave them an edge at long ranges. In addition, the Stalin carried only twenty-eight rounds of main gun ammunition, limiting its effectiveness in sustained combat situations.[22]

Above: German soldiers pose with a knocked-out T-34 tank.

Right: Soviet prisoners. Red Army soldiers risked retribution from the Soviet government for surrendering.

Above: A Soviet KV-2 tank.
Below: Soviet tanks captured by the Germans before they could even detrain.

German soldiers with a captured Soviet artillery piece.

SOVIET DOMINANCE

1945 on the Eastern Front

Jan 12–Feb 2	Soviet Vistula–Oder offensive
Feb 4–11	Yalta Conference
Feb 13	Soviets take Budapest
Feb 13–May 6	Siege of Breslau
Mar 6–16	Operation Spring Awakening (Hungary)
Apr 2–13	Soviet Vienna offensive
Apr 16–19	Battle of the Seelow Heights
Apr 16–May 2	Battle of Berlin
Apr 30	Hitler commits suicide
May 6–11	Soviet Prague offensive
May 8	VE Day

On the German side, the latest versions of the Panther, the *Ausführung A* and *Ausführung G*, had finally reached an acceptable level of reliability. In addition, new armored vehicles like the *Jagdpanther* ("Hunting Panther"), with its superb 88mm main gun, and the massive Panzer VI, *Ausführung B "Königstiger,"* mounting a similar weapon, were all powerful vehicles, but they were produced in far too

few numbers to have any significant effect on the course of the war.[23]

Pour on the shells . . . no more talks. Storm the place."

> *Chuikov, May 1, 1945*

While foot infantry continued to hold the majority of the line, the corset stays of German operations were the panzer and *Panzergrenadier* divisions, whose role had fundamentally changed. From once being the spearheads of the offense, they were now defensive "fire brigades," being dispatched to threatened parts of the front or where Red Army mobile forces, usually tank armies, had broken through. Even employed in that role, their effectiveness was often limited, since Allied bombing efforts against fuel-production facilities were starting to have significant effect, with the size and scope of German operations oftentimes dictated by how much fuel was available, even when responding to emergency situations.

Faced with an ever-dwindling manpower pool, the incessant demands for more forces on the part of Hitler, and the inability of German industry to keep up with demand, the force-structure branch of the German Army resorted to

With some help from the engineers, a German tank travels across the often tricky Russian terrain.

SOVIET DOMINANCE

several organizational tricks in an effort to maintain the force. For the armor branch, this resulted in fewer equipment and manpower authorizations for most formations. The resulting organizations were "leaner and meaner" in theory, but the inability of German industry to keep up with fielding demands meant that many elements were chronically short of vehicles. An important exception was the divisional reconnaissance element, the *Panzer-Aufklärungs-Abteilung,*

The varieties of German transport, to include captured vehicles, a logistics nightmare.

which actually gained additional firepower, armor, and maneuverability in the new armored reconnaissance structure of the *Model 1943 Panzer-Division.*[24] Since these battalions were increasingly being called upon to fight in an effort to reconnoiter and their function as a command & control element for rearguard operations had increased exponentially, the steps taken to beef up the force were a natural progression.[25]

A S WITH THE WEST, THE EASTERN
Front in 1944 saw the beginning of the knockout blows that
would be the death knell for the
Third Reich. The first half of the
year was marked by some continued give and take and, until the
middle of 1944, *Heeresgruppe
Mitte* had defeated all previous Red
Army attempts to advance, where
the front lines had barely changed
since late 1943. It was expected

that a renewed Soviet offensive
would occur in the South, and this
assessment was reinforced by a brilliant deception plan (*maskirovka*)
on the part of the Soviets, that convinced the German high command
that this was indeed the case. Of the
thirty panzer and *Panzergrenadier*
divisions at the front, twenty-four
were concentrated in the South.

Operation Bagration commenced
on 22 June, exactly three years

Roads on the Eastern Front ranged from dusty to muddy to frozen.

SOVIET DOMINANCE

A Panzer III on the Eastern Front, probably in the southern sector, given the mountains in the background.

after the commencement of Operation Barbarossa. The Red Army committed nineteen combined-arms and two tank armies, comprised of 1,400,000 men, more than 5,000 tanks and assault guns, and 31,000 field pieces and heavy mortars against *Heeresgruppe Mitte* alone. Those field armies had the support of more than 5,000 aircraft. The primary aim was not so much to liberate territory but to completely destroy *Heeresgruppe Mitte*, with its 1,200,000 men, 900 tanks and assault guns, and 9,500 pieces of artillery. *Luftwaffe* support amounted to around 1,300 aircraft, with perhaps 50% of them operational.

Georgy Zhukov Career Highlights

1896	Born in Russia
1915	Conscripted into World War I
1918–21	Russian Civil War for Bolsheviks
1923	Commander, 39th Cavalry Regiment
1930	Commander, 2nd Cavalry Brigade
1931	Assistant Inspector of Cavalry of the Red Army
1933	Commander, 4th Cavalry Division
1937	Commander, 3rd Cavalry Corps
1938–39	Commander, First Soviet Mongolian Army Group (Khalkhyn Gol)
Feb 1941	Chief of Red Army General Staff
July 1941	Removed as Chief of General Staff
Sept 1941	Commander, Leningrad Front
Aug 1942	Deputy Commander-in-Chief, including defense of Stalingrad
Jan 1943	Operation Iskra
July 1943	Battle of Kursk
March 1944	Commander, 1st Ukrainian Front
June 1944	Operation Bagration (1st and 2nd Belorussian Fronts)
Nov 1944–May 1945	Commander, 1st Belorussian Front (Vistula-Oder offensive, Battle of Berlin)
May 1945	Witnesses signing of surrender
May 1945–Apr 1946	Commander, Soviet Occupation Zone in Germany
July–Aug 1945	Participates in Potsdam Conference
1953	Deputy Defense Minister
1956	Receives fourth Hero of the Soviet Union award
1974	Dies

A Soviet T26 tank in whitewash snow disruptive camouflage pattern.

There's no need for you to try and teach me. . . . I've had more practical experience than any gentleman of the General Staff could ever hope to have."

➣ *Hitler to Guderian*

The German troop dispositions could almost be characterized as suicidal, with large and virtually immobile garrisons stationed, at Hitler's insistence, in the "fortress cities" of Bobruisk, Mogilev, Orsha, and Vitebsk. These groups positively invited encirclement and subsequent destruction. This occurred without achieving any slowing down, let alone the defeating, of the Soviet offensive. So overwhelming and rapid was the Soviet offensive, that the panzer divisions in the South were almost powerless to intervene as *Heeresgruppe Mitte* quickly collapsed, its demise hastened by Hitler's customary no-retreat orders. By the end of August, as the Soviet offensive finally wound down, the German field-army group had ceased to exist as an effective force, suffering an estimated 300,000 killed, wounded, and missing—a disaster greater

Above: A Maxim antiaircraft gun.
Right: A German forward observer,
ready to call in artillery strikes.

than Stalingrad and Germany's
greatest defeat of the war. The Red
Army reached the border of Prussia
in the North and, in the South, was
only 100 kilometers from Warsaw.

We shall exact a brutal
revenge for
everything."

➢ *Zhukov*

From July to November 1944, the Red Army advanced through the Baltic States, isolating the *16. Armee* and *18. Armee* of *Heeresgruppe Nord*, with their thirty-three divisions, in the Courland Peninsula.

The *Kriegsmarine* was able to evacuate substantial numbers of men and materiel, but twenty-one divisions—189,000 troops—remained in *Heeresgruppe Kurland*, as it was redesignated on

Soviet prisoners.

26 January 1945. This grouping was subjected to repeated, intensive attempts by the Soviets to liquidate the pocket. However, these attacks were all defeated, inflicting huge casualties on the Red Army, and the garrison did not finally surrender until 9 May 1945. While some sources indicate that the defense offered by *Heeresgruppe Kurland* tied up significant numbers of Soviet forces and resources, others convincingly argue that the encircled German field army group could have better served the Reich as part of the main defensive effort along the German frontier.

Red Army soldier! You are now on German soil. The hour of revenge has struck!"

> *Soviet poster*

Although the Germans had fortified the front between the Vistula and Oder with seven defensive zones some 300 miles deep, they had neither the troops to fully man them nor the artillery and antitank guns to reinforce them. The whole German defensive structure in the East was falling apart. The Soviet forces were far too strong, and their commanders were now highly skilled

A crew loads a 5cm PaK 38 antitank gun.

SOVIET DOMINANCE

"Europe Will Never Be Russian"

As the *Third Reich crumbled around him, Adolf Hitler issued Führer Order 74 on 15 April 1945. Note the similarity to Stalin's Order No. 270 of Aug 1941, in which the Soviet premier, while German armies flooded the Soviet Union, threatened death for officers who surrendered.*

For the last time our deadly enemies the Jewish Bolsheviks have launched their massive forces to the attack. Their aim is to reduce Germany to ruins and to exterminate our people. Many of you soldiers in the East already know the fate which threatens, above all, German women, girls, and children. While the old men and children will be murdered, the women and girls will be reduced to barrack-room whores. The remainder will be marched off to Siberia. . . .

This time the Bolshevik will meet the ancient fate of Asia—he must and shall bleed to death before the capital of the German Reich. Whoever fails in his duty at this moment behaves as a traitor to our people. The regiment or division which abandons its position acts so disgracefully that it must be ashamed before the women and children who are withstanding the terror of bombing in our cities. Above all, be on your guard against the few treacherous officers and soldiers who, in order to preserve their pitiful lives, fight against us in Russian pay, perhaps even wearing German uniform. Anyone ordering you to retreat will, unless you know him well personally, be immediately arrested and, if necessary, killed on the spot, no matter what rank he may hold. If every soldier on the Eastern Front does his duty in the days and weeks which lie ahead, the last assault of Asia will crumple, just as the invasion by our enemies in the West will finally fail, in spite of everything.

Berlin remains German, Vienna will be German again, and Europe will never be Russian. ■

Red Army troops storm into battle.

at directing mobile operations. In stark contrast, German generals were continually hamstrung by Hitler's increasingly inane orders to hold at all costs. In many cases, command was being dictated by how sycophantic toward Hitler the commanding officer was and not on any inherent military skills. Ground down by the massive Allied round-the-clock air offensive over Europe, the *Luftwaffe* could no longer provide even minimal air support. The apparent success of the few German armored counterattacks was illusory and, in the long run, achieved nothing.

Warsaw, or what was left of it after the failed Polish Home Army uprising, fell on 17 January 1945, as German commanders disobeyed Hitler's order to hold and wisely withdrew. In a brilliant encircling maneuver by the Soviets, the vital

Above: German soldiers pause for a meal.

Left: The legendary German 88mm flak gun.

Little remains of this town except the church.

Silesian industrial region was captured intact. After a 500-kilometer advance in two weeks, the 1st Byelorussian Front had established several bridgeheads across the last river obstacle before Berlin, the Oder River, only some 60 kilometers from the city.

In the extreme South, the Rumanian front, which had been calm for four months, suddenly exploded on 20 August 1944. The 2nd and

3rd Ukrainian Fronts attacked Frießner's *Heeresgruppe Südukraine* and trapped the eighteen German divisions of the 6. *Armee,* as well as the Rumanian 3rd Army. On 23 August, Rumania switched sides and declared war on Germany. On 8 September, Soviet forces crossed the Bulgarian border, with Bulgaria also declaring war on Germany the next day. The remnants of *Heeresgruppe Südukraine,*

German Instrument of Surrender

At Berlin on May 8, 1945, the German High Command signed the instrument of surrender, witnessed by Georgy Zhukov, Arthur Tedder, Jean de Lattre de Tassigny, and Carl Spaatz.

1. We the undersigned, acting by authority of the German High Command, hereby surrender unconditionally to the Supreme Commander, Allied Expeditionary Force and simultaneously to the Supreme High Command of the Red Army all forces on land, sea, and in the air who are at this date under German control.

2. The German High Command will at once issue orders to all German military, naval and air authorities and to all forces under German control to cease active operations at 2301 hours Central European time on 8th May 1945, to remain in the positions occupied at that time and to disarm completely, handing over their weapons and equipment to the local allied commanders or officers designated by Representatives of the Allied Supreme Commands. No ship, vessel, or aircraft is to be scuttled, or any damage done to their hull, machinery or equipment, and also to machines of all kinds, armament, apparatus, and all the technical means of prosecution of war in general.

3. The German High Command will at once issue to the appropriate commanders, and ensure the carrying out of any further orders issued by the Supreme Commander, Allied Expeditionary Force and by the Supreme High Command of the Red Army.

4. This act of military surrender is without prejudice to, and will be superseded by any general instrument of surrender imposed by, or on behalf of the United Nations and applicable to Germany and the German armed forces as a whole.

5. In the event of the German High Command or any of the forces under their control failing to act in accordance with this Act of Surrender, the Supreme Commander, Allied Expeditionary Force and the Supreme High Command of the Red Army will take such punitive or other action as they deem appropriate.

6. This act is drawn up in the English, Russian and German languages. The English and Russian are the only authentic texts. ∎

German assault guns.

renamed *Heeresgruppe Süd*, and Wöhler's understrength *8. Armee* were pushed back into Hungary.

As the Red Army pushed into Hungary, it suffered one of its few significant late-war setbacks. The Debrecen Operation (6–28 October) was initiated with the intention of Malinovsky's 2nd Ukrainian Front destroying Frießner's *Heeresgruppe Süd*. This led to a number of large armored engagements from 10–29 October.

The Commander-in-Chief of the 6. Armee, *General der Artillerie* Fretter-Pico, ordered his *1. Panzer-Division* and *13. Panzer-Division* to encircle and destroy Group Pliyev's advancing III Corps, consisting of the 4th and 5th Cavalry Divisions and the 23rd Tank Division. The *23. Panzer-Division* and *Panzergrenadier-Division* "*Feldherrnhalle*"[26] were to act as reinforcements and flank protection. By 12 October, trapped Soviet elements broke out of the thinly held encirclement and Group Pliyev was able to capture Debrecen on 20 October. Rather than moving back to defensive positions, Frießner was convinced by his Chief-of-Staff, *Generalmajor* Grolman, to counterattack instead. While Wöhler's *8. Armee* took the Soviet forces in the flank, Fretter-Pico's main forces—the *1. Panzer-Division* and the *23. Panzer-Division*, spearheaded by *schwere Panzer-Abteilung 503* and its "King Tiger" tanks—attacked eastward once again, trapping Group Pliyev.

It is now time for our soldiers to issue their own justice."

➤ *Vasilievsky*

This time, there was no breakout, and relief efforts by Malinovsky's forces were decisively defeated in a veritable storm of artillery and particularly effective tank and antitank gunfire, inflicting significant tank losses. By 29 October, the trapped formations destroyed their heavy weapons and broke out on foot. Group Pliyev suffered some 25,000 casualties in killed, wounded, and missing, along with 360 tanks and more than 1,000 artillery pieces,

A Soviet village burns.

antitank guns, and heavy mortars captured or destroyed. This was the last successful large-scale German counterattack on the Eastern Front.

For the Soviets, however, this was only a temporary setback, as the operations to take Budapest were launched on 29 October. By

26 December, after particularly
heavy fighting, Budapest was
surrounded. Six divisions were
trapped—two armored (*"Feldherrnhalle"* and the *13. Panzer-Division*), two Hungarian infantry
(10th and 22nd) and two *SS* cavalry
(the 8th and the 22nd)—plus a

miscellany of infantry and other
armored units. In all, about 70,000
personnel were surrounded, of
which approximately 55% were
Hungarian. Despite three relief
attempts—Konrad I, Konrad II, and
Konrad III—featuring strong *SS*
and Army armored units, the Soviet

defensive ring was too formidable to be broken, despite exceptional efforts by the German elements. The desperate defenders of Budapest could not hold out for long against the overwhelmingly superior Red Army forces, and the city finally fell on 13 February, most of it totally destroyed.

The Soviet forces reached Lake Balaton on 5 March and Hitler ordered a counteroffensive called *Frühlingserwachen* ("Spring Awakening"). The *6. SS-Panzer-Armee* attacked from north of the lake and the *2. Panzer-Armee* from the south against Tolbukhin's 3rd Ukrainian Front. Despite initial success—an advance of 32 kilometers in the first twenty-four hours—the attack slowed to a crawl due to a combination of the muddy spring conditions and Tolbukhin's hastily prepared defensive positions, some up to 45 kilometers in depth. The brutal fighting continued unabated for ten days, with both sides suffering considerable tank and personnel casualties, before the Germans, after coming within 24 kilometers of Budapest, broke off the offensive on 15 March, conserving what was left of their armor for the final defense of the rapidly diminishing Reich. By 4 April, the 3rd Ukrainian Front was within 8 kilometers of Vienna,

and by the 13th of that month, had taken total control of the city.

For the Berlin Operation, Zhukov's 1st Belorussian Front, Rokossovsky's 2nd Belorussian Front and Konev's 1st Ukrainian Front consisted of 2,500,000 troops, 6,250 tanks and assault guns and 45,000 artillery pieces and rocket launchers. These were supported by 7,500 aircraft. *Heeresgruppe Weichsel* and *Heeresgruppe Mitte*, the main opposing forces, deployed 770,000 troops, including the Berlin garrison, which consisted mainly of boys of the Hitler Youth and old men of the *Volksturm* ("Peoples' Militia"). They were supported by 1,500 tanks and assault guns, with the *Luftwaffe* somehow scraping together about 500 operational aircraft, mainly fighters.[27]

Against such overpowering numbers, the issue was never in doubt. The divisions manning the commanding Seelow Heights offered stiff resistance, with the main armored opposition coming from the Panthers of *Panzer-Division "Müncheberg"* along with the *Königstiger* tanks of *schwere Panzer-Abteilung 512*. The heavy flak batteries that had relocated from Berlin also took a heavy toll of Soviet armor, with even the IS-2 Stalin formations suffering harsh losses.

Stalin's Victory Speech

On 9 May 1945, Stalin broadcast the following from Moscow:

The great day of victory over Germany has come. Fascist Germany, forced to her knees by the Red Army and the troops of our Allies, has acknowledged herself defeated and declared unconditional surrender. . . .

Being aware of the wolfish habits of the German ringleaders, who regard treaties and agreements as empty scraps of paper, we have no reason to trust their words. However, this morning, in pursuance of the act of surrender, the German troops began to lay down their arms and surrender to our troops *en masse*. This is no longer an empty scrap of paper. This is actual surrender of Germany's armed forces. True, one group of German troops in the area of Czechoslovakia is still evading surrender. But I trust that the Red Army will be able to bring it to its senses. . . .

The great sacrifices we made in the name of the freedom and independence of our Motherland, the incalculable privations and sufferings experienced by our people in the course of the war, the intense work in the rear and at the front, placed on the altar of the Motherland, have not been in vain, and have been crowned by complete victory over the enemy. The age–long struggle of the Slav peoples for their existence and their independence has ended in victory over the German invaders and German tyranny.

Henceforth the great banner of the freedom of the peoples and peace among peoples will fly over Europe. . . .

Glory to our heroic Red Army, which upheld the independence of our Motherland and won victory over the enemy! Glory to our great people, the people victorious! Eternal glory to the heroes who fell in the struggle against the enemy and gave their lives for the freedom and happiness of our people! ■

The Seelow Heights took two days to break through, from 16–17 April. After surprisingly stubborn German opposition, it was only on 26 April that 500,000 troops, supported by 12,700 artillery pieces, 2,000 rocket launchers, and 1,500 tanks and assault guns, attacked the city center. Despite their overwhelming superiority, the Red Army suffered heavy infantry and armored vehicle casualties in the vicious street fighting, with the final fighting for the symbolic *Reichstag* lasting from 30 April to 2 May. On 2 May, the commander of the Berlin garrison, *General der Artillerie* Weidling surrendered the city. Just like Berlin, the Third Reich was now shattered almost beyond recognition.

Epilogue: The Costs of War

THE EASTERN FRONT JUSTIFIABLY has received the reputation as the largest and bloodiest theater of operations in World War II. Once combat was joined in June 1941, the majority of the entire German Army was committed to operations in the East. In 1942, this figure rose to more than 80%, but even at the height of the multi-front war following the Invasion of Normandy in June 1944 by the Western Allies, Germany still never had less than 60% of its ground forces committed to fighting the Soviets. By the end of the war, the Soviets still enjoyed an almost 4-to-1 manpower advantage over the Germans, despite the continued emphasis on the Eastern Front by Hitler and the German Armed Forces High Command.

Casualties, both civilian and military, were enormous on both sides. Of the two main combatants, the Soviets suffered the most, with nearly 35,000,000 casualties suffered, of which 42%—almost 15,000,000 personnel—were listed as killed, missing, or captured. Another 29,000,000 civilians are estimated to have perished as well. In contrast, German losses were less catastrophic in comparison to the Soviets, but enormous nonetheless. Of the nearly 14,000,000 soldiers listed as killed, missing, captured, or disabled in the entire war, almost 11,000,000 were in the east. These figures do not count the nearly 2,000,000 men lost by Germany's allies as well, nor do they include German civilian deaths suffered at the hands of a vengeful Red Army when it finally breached the German frontier in late 1944.

The ferocity of the fighting can also be measured by the materiel losses. It is estimated that almost 43,000 tanks and other armored fighting vehicles were lost on the Eastern Front by the German Army and its allies. For their part, the Soviets suffered the loss of more than twice that number, nearly 97,000 in all. While Soviet combat losses in aircraft were nearly three-fold those of the *Luftwaffe*—some 46,000 versus 16,000—the total losses by the German Air Force were almost as high as the Soviets.

German infantry on the move, while Russia burns.

In addition, there were other costs that rarely get considered and which affected the Soviet Union for decades after the war: the displacement and frequent homelessness of large segments of the population; the destruction of entire population centers and supporting infrastructure; economic dislocation; loss of livestock and agrarian capacity; involuntary migrations, etc.

The post-war landscape of Europe was changed in ways that few could have imagined at the start of the conflict. According to historian David Glantz:

> During its Great Patriotic War, the Red Army defeated the Twentieth Century's most formidable armed force after suffering the equivalent of what the Soviets later described as the effects of an atomic war. By virtue of the Red Army's four-year struggle, Hitler's Third *Reich*, which was supposed to last for 1,000 years, perished in only 12 years, and *Nazi* domination of Europe ended. By war's end, the Red Army had emerged as the world's premier killing machine. Tragically, however, this killing machine proved as deadly for the Red Army's soldiers as it did for those serving the Axis powers. After war's end and by virtue of its performance in the war, the Soviet Union quickly emerged as the dominant power in Eurasia and one of the world's two super-powers.[28]

Notes

1. David M. Glantz, "The Soviet-German War, 1941–1945: Myths and Realities: A Survey Essay," A Paper Presented as the 20th Anniversary Distinguished Lecture at the Strom Thurmond Institute of Government and Public Affairs, Clemson University on 11 October 2001 at Clemson, South Carolina. Downloaded as a PDF from http://sti.clemson.edu/publications-mainmenu-38/commentaries-mainmenu-211/cat_view/33-strom-thurmond-institute/153-sti-publications-by-subject-area/158-history. In particular, see Figure 1 on page 7.
2. Glantz, Figure 2, page 9. Those numbers represent those serving at the time and do not reflect the constant turbulence in the end strength of the force due to casualties, transfers, and the like. Thus, the total number who served is considerably higher than a mere snapshot in time would indicate. These figures also do not represent the number of foreign formations and individuals that constituted the *Axis* Forces, to include regular military formations from Italy, Rumania, and Hungary, as well as volunteers from almost all European countries serving within the ranks of "foreign legions" of the German Army and the *Waffen-SS*, Hitler's Praetorian Guard.
3. The standard name by which the Soviets referred to the war, even though the concept of "patriotism" was antithetical to Communist ideology. In an effort to rally his nation to the concept of "total war," Stalin was forced to appeal to nationalism and patriotism, in addition to other concessions to the bourgeois past (e.g., reintroduction of rank titles within the military).
4. Glantz, pp. 12–13.
5. There is some debate as to whether the delayed start date for Barbarossa affected the outcome of the campaign, but the German military effort in the Balkans was essentially a sideshow that did not involve a significant amount of force structure. Some also argue that an earlier start date for Barbarossa would have forced the Germans to start their campaign against the Soviet Union during the annual "mud season."

6. The precursor to the *Waffen-SS*, an organization also surrounded by its own mystique and hagiography. From a relatively small but elite formation designed to be the personal bodyguard of Hitler, it grew to a large, multinational force by war's end numbering more than 500,000 men. Some of the last casualties of the war were sustained by French volunteers of the *Charlemagne* Division fighting to defend Berlin.

7. Among the most numerous armored fighting vehicles were 11,000 T26s and 6,000 BT fast tanks. The former was based on a British Vickers design and the latter had the unique suspension developed by American entrepreneur and developer J. Walter Christie. Both tanks were essentially obsolete by the start of the war, but that was also true of the *Panzertruppe*. Some 500 KV medium and heavy tanks were also available to Soviet mechanized forces, most of them the lighter and more nimble KV1, which was armed with a 76.2mm main gun and heavily armored. The KV1 weighed 47 tons and had a maximum road speed of only 21 mph (34kph) and cross country speed of 10 mph (16kph). It was pretty much a lumbering beast at the best of times and easily outmaneuvered by the lighter German armor, but destroying it was another matter entirely! As with most major conflicts, the war saw exponential advances in the development and fielding of weapons and technology both in the East and the West.

8. The argument being that combat forces have to be forward deployed in order to conduct offensive operations. Had a purely defensive posture been maintained, the combat elements would have been positioned further back and "layered" in successive defensive belts. As a result of the poor positioning of the Soviet forces, they practically invited encirclement by the rapidly moving armored forces employed in the first echelon of the German attack force. The counterargument runs that the Soviet forces were forward deployed and waiting for the construction of the new "Molotov Line" (named after the Soviet foreign minister) to be completed prior to occupation.

9. Despite the horrendous casualties, the number of Soviet divisions had actually increased to 212 by mid-July although only about 90 were anywhere near full strength. The Germans had initially estimated a total of 200 Soviet divisions capable of combat operations, but by August the number had risen to no less than 360. These numbers would continue to rise into the winter. One caveat must be applied, however: On average, Soviet divisions were only about half the strength of a German division.

10. Stalin and his high command had wanted to start counteroffensive operations almost from the very beginning, but they were unable to do so, primarily due to the speed of the Germans and the slowness of his own chain-of-command to react and adapt to changing situations.
11. While the force structure was often adjusted, the battalions moved around were rarely at full strength. In fact, Hitler rarely approved the complete disbanding of formations that had been effectively wiped out. Instead, forces were taken from other sources—other divisions, the training base, etc. —to bring the decimated forces back up to a semblance of strength. Forces that had been rendered completely combat ineffective were generally pulled out of the line for reconstitution in the rear or even back in Germany. Needless to say, such turbulence took its toll on unit cohesiveness, but it helped mask the mauling that some units and organizations had taken in the course of the fighting. Other force structure sleights-of-hand were also employed to keep the force at "full strength," mostly in the restructuring of tables of organization & equipment to make smaller organizations and reduce the "logistical tail."
12. Some question whether the Soviet Union could have even won the war on its front without the assistance provided by the United States through Lend-Lease. In all, some $11 billion in aid was provided (1940s dollars), including 400,000 tactical wheeled vehicles, 12,000 armored vehicles (among them, more than 4,000 M4 Sherman medium tanks) and 11,400 aircraft. While the armored fighting vehicles were a mixed blessing to most Soviet tankers, there is no question that the trucks and jeeps helped immensely in the Soviet war effort.
13. Army Group "Don" was a short-lived field formation that was primarily formed to give Manstein a headquarters for the forces at his disposal in the effort to thwart the Soviet offensives. It was formed from the headquarters of the *11. Armee* in late November 1942 and was later dissolved in February 1943, when it was consolidated with *Heeresgruppe B* and redesignated as the new *Heeresgruppe Süd*. As the Eastern Front grew ever more chaotic for the Germans, more and more field-army groups were created and dissolved in response to ever-changing situations.
14. Although the first-line *SS* divisions are often assumed to be *Panzer* divisions, they did not formally achieve that status until 1944, when they were authorized a full armored regiment. In fact, they only started to receive tank battalions in 1942. Organizationally, the *SS* divisions

were essentially the same as their army counterparts, although some argue that they received preferential treatment in the replacement of lost materiel and were fielded with the latest equipment first. As with most elite formations, the argument can also be made that enlisted personnel in them could serve as noncommissioned officers in "normal" elements, thus hurting the force as a whole.

15. An *SS* rank, roughly equivalent to the German *Generalleutnant* or a Lieutenant General in British and US usage.

16. Also debuting at the battle was the *Ferdinand* tank destroyer, another armored fighting vehicle upon which great hopes rested. Armed with a highly effective 88mm main gun and protected by armor that was almost impregnable at the time, it nonetheless also suffered from considerable teething problems, primarily due to the fact that *Professor Doktor* Porsche's design was overengineered (e.g., a unique for its time petro-electrical drive train). More units were lost to mechanical failure than combat action. Although it continued to be employed until the end of the war—overhauled vehicles were upgraded and redesignated as the *Elefant* ("Elephant")—it never really entered into series production, with less than 100 being manufactured.

17. The engagement has also spawned its own cottage industry, including one of the largest military-history books ever. See Christopher A. Lawrence, *Kursk: The Battle of Prokhorovka* (Sheridan, CO: Aberdeen Books, 2015). A single volume treatise on the fighting at Prokhorovka, Mr. Lawrence's book numbers some 1,652 pages. How the book came to be written is outlined in a downloadable PDF (www.aberdeenbookstore.com/LiteratureRetrieve.aspx?ID=228520): Did I Just Write the Largest History Book Ever?

18. While German tactical combat losses were considerably less than the Soviets', the aggregate losses were considerable, since they had to abandon the battlefield and could not recover many vehicles that had broken down or were temporarily non-operational due to battlefield damage. It was a problem that would plague the Germans for the rest of the war, compounded by chronic fuel shortages from about the middle of 1944 onward.

19. It should be noted that German field armies were theoretically twice as large as the equivalent Soviet formation, but that none of the German formations were at full strength.

20. Although many historians praise the Germans for being able to replace losses in personnel relatively quickly and reconstituting combat elements, many of those replacements came from the logistics or training base or forced transfers from superfluous elements of the *Luftwaffe* and *Kriegsmarine* (Navy), which were of doubtful value in combat line units, except as cannon fodder.

21. More than 4,000 wounded were flown out.

22. The basic load of ammunition was usually twenty high-explosive rounds and eight armor-piercing rounds. Contributing to its limitations in tank-versus-tank combat was the slow rate of fire of the main gun (separately cased ammunition). Nonetheless, it was a feared opponent for all German tank crews. The development of other types of armored fighting vehicles also continued apace, with most being continuously uparmored and upgunned. Examples include the SU-85/100 tank destroyers, the SU-76 light infantry support vehicles, and SU-122/152 and ISU-122/152 heavy assault guns. (In each case, the number represents the caliber of the main gun). All of these vehicles were manufactured in substantial numbers, with some 4,500 of the ISU-122/152 being produced.

23. Significant improvements were also made to other types of armored fighting vehicles as well, with the *Sturmgeschütz IV* assault gun joining the *Sturmgeschütz III* in providing support to the hard-pressed infantry, while new families of tank destroyer vehicles were fielded as well. In almost all cases, vehicles were either uparmored or upgunned or both. Experiments were also conducted with new technologies, such as remote/radio control, television cameras, and night-vision optics, but none of these really ever reached true "field ready" status.

24. The battalions continued with a five-company model, fielding two scout companies (generally one with wheeled armored cars and the other with light reconnaissance halftracks), two light reconnaissance companies (also mounted on halftracks) and an armored heavy company, which featured halftracks as the primary means of movement or maneuver for the battalion's heavy weaponry. In addition, each battalion was allocated a heavy armored car platoon, which had six of the *Sd.Kfz. 233* armored cars armed with the short 75mm main gun. The use of the light and medium *SPW* throughout the battalion saw considerable improvement in the ability to protect the force. In addition, the fact that each halftracked vehicle generally had a light pedestal-mounted machine gun, substantially increased firepower. Of course, these were theoretical

constructs that were never fully attained, with many battalions maintaining a hodgepodge of vehicles, but it was a step in improving deficiencies that had long been identified in the organization of the armored reconnaissance force.

25. Because of their increased maneuverability, firepower, and armor, the battalions were often seen as miniature mechanized infantry regiments. In fact, because of their large allocations of halftracks, they often had more firepower and offensive striking power, if not an equal amount of manpower. Consequently, they increasingly began to be used as fire brigades as well, since they could be shunted across the battlefield with relative ease and the inherent *Reitergeist* ("cavalry spirit") of the formation allowed it to move, regroup, and change missions quickly and effectively.

26. Like many reconstituted divisions, the latter was considerably understrength and had no tanks. The division's antitank battalion had been issued assault guns, which represented the only armored strength of the organization. It was also shorthanded with only two batteries instead of the theoretical three. This type of stop-gap organization was oftentimes the norm at this stage of the war.

27. By 10 April, only a total of 2,200 German tanks and assault guns were available for combat operations along the entire Eastern Front. Most of these were assault guns (*Sturmgeschütz IIIs* and *IVs*) and tank destroyers (e.g., *Jagdpanzer 38(t)s*). For the defense of Berlin, many armored fighting vehicles were employed as bunkers, situated along intersections or other areas where there were good fields of fire.

28. Glantz, p. 15.

Suggested Reading

The Battle of Kursk by David M. Glantz and Jonathan M. House. Authoritative reconstruction of the massive battle during the summer of 1943.

Bloodlands by Timothy Snyder. A shattering analysis of how Hitler and Stalin were flip sides of the same coin of mass political-ideological killing.

The Fall of Berlin 1945 by Antony Beevor. Vivid account of the brutal final phase of the Eastern Front.

Frontsoldaten by Stephen G. Fritz. Deeply researched description of life in the German Army, relying heavily on the words of the soldiers themselves.

Hitler by Ian Kershaw. *The* biography of Adolf Hitler-—magisterial, definitive—available in two volumes or in a one-volume abridgment.

Ivan's War by Catherine Merridale. Gracefully written portrait of what it was like to be a common soldier in the Red Army.

The 900 Days by Harrison E. Salisbury. The classic account of the siege of Leningrad.

Operation Barbarossa by Christian Hartmann. A sparkling (and misleadingly titled) history of Germany's war in the East—in fewer than 200 pages.

Ordinary Men by Christopher R. Browning. Influential, insightful account of how average German draftees became killers in the Holocaust.

The Road to Stalingrad and *The Road to Berlin* by John Erickson. Dense, dry, but detailed, these narratives remain one of the best accounts of the Eastern Front.

Stalin by Stephen Kotkin. This trilogy awaits its final installment covering the war years and the early Cold War, but it will surely be the definitive biography of Josef Stalin for decades.

Stalingrad by Antony Beevor. Evocative retelling of one of World War II's major turning points.

The Third Reich at War by Richard J. Evans. Monumental account of Nazi Germany at war: on the battlefield, on the homefront, and against the Jews.

Warsaw 1944 by Alexandra Richie. Painstaking account of a city's agony.

When Titans Clashed by David M. Glantz and Jonathan M. House. A military history of the Red Army during World War II.

A World at Arms by Gerhard Weinberg. The gold standard in one-volume histories of the war, combining diplomatic, military, political, and economic perspectives.